Boat-Mania!

University Branch

MAY 3 0 2007

By Steve Parker

Gareth Stevens Publishing
A WORLD ALMANAC EDUCATION GROUP COMPANY

Please visit our web site at: www.garethstevens.com
For a free color catalog describing Gareth Stevens Publishing's list
of high-quality books and multimedia programs, call 1-800-542-2595 (USA)
or 1-800-387-3178 (Canada). Gareth Stevens Publishing's fax: (414) 332-3567.

Library of Congress Cataloging-in-Publication Data

Parker, Steve.
    Boat-mania! / by Steve Parker. — North American ed.
      p. cm. — (Vehicle-mania!)
    Includes index.
    Contents: Drag boat — Chinese junk — Submersible — Tall ship — Racing yacht — Research ship —
Fireboat — Aircraft carrier — Supertanker — Jet ski — Ferry — Luxury liner — Rescue boat.
    ISBN 0-8368-3782-7 (lib. bdg.)
    1. Boats and boating—Juvenile literature. 2. Ships—Juvenile literature. [1. Boats and boating.
2. Ships.] I. Title. II. Series.
    VM150.P8596   2003
    623.8'2—dc21
                                                                             2003043920

This North American edition first published in 2004 by
Gareth Stevens Publishing
A WRC Media Company
330 West Olive Street, Suite 100
Milwaukee, Wisconsin 53212

This U.S. edition copyright © 2004 by Gareth Stevens Inc. Original edition copyright © 2003 ticktock Entertainment Ltd.
First published in Great Britain in 2003 by ticktock Media Ltd., Unit 2, Orchard Business Centre, North Farm Road,
Tunbridge Wells, Kent, TN2 3XF, United Kingdom.

We would like to thank: Tim Bones, Keith Faulkner of Janes, and Elizabeth Wiggans.

Gareth Stevens Editor: Jim Mezzanotte
Gareth Stevens Art Direction: Tammy West

Photo credits: Alamy: P6-7 all, P21t, P25t. Beken of Cowes: P12c, P18-19c, British Antarctic Survey: P14-15, all Corbis: P8-9c,
P16-17 all, P19t, P20c. Hawkes Ocean Technologies: P9t, John Clark Photography: P4-5c, RNLI: P28-29 Stena: P24c World of
Residensea: P26-27 all Yamaha: P23t.

Printed in the United States of America

2 3 4 5 6 7 8 9 09 08 07 06 05

CONTENTS

DRAG BOAT

Drag boats are incredibly fast. These single-seater racing boats have huge, powerful engines, and they shoot like rockets across the water. *California Quake*, for example, has reached speeds of 230 miles (370 kilometers) per hour!

Did You Know?

Drag boat racing is very popular and usually attracts large crowds of people.

California Quake **has a 5,000-horsepower (hp) engine. It is the first boat in the world to travel 1/4 mile (400 meters) in under 5 seconds.**

Oxygen is supplied to the driver's helmet. If the boat crashes, the driver will be able to breathe while waiting to be rescued.

FACTS AND STATS

First Year: 1999

Origin: United States

Length:
25 feet (7.6 meters)

Width:
12 feet (3.7 m)

Maximum Weight:
5.2 tons (4.7 metric tons)

Fuel Capacity:
5 gallons (19 liters)

Load: 1 pilot

Engines:
One nitromethane
engine rated at 5,000 hp

Maximum Speed:
230 miles (370 km) per hour

The driver sits inside a special capsule that has a **roll cage** for protection. During a high-speed crash, the capsule breaks free of the boat.

CHINESE JUNK

The Chinese junk is one of the world's oldest boat designs. The first junks sailed over 2,000 years ago. Later, junks were used for trading goods in many different places. The *June Lee* is one of many modern junks. Today, junks still carry goods — from rice and timber to computers and cars!

The sails are made of woven fibers, such as **linen**. They are supported by a frame made from long poles of bamboo or wood.

Did You Know?

The name "junk" probably comes from the Chinese word *jung*, which means "floating house."

The **hull** of a junk is divided into separate spaces by **bulkheads**. If water leaks into one space, it cannot spread to another space, so the ship stays afloat.

Today, many junks have engines in addition to sails. They also have equipment that uses **satellites** to help pilots find their way.

SUBMERSIBLE

Did You Know?

A trip in a submersible down to the sunken wreck of the giant ocean liner *Titanic* costs about $40,000.

Submersibles are like miniature submarines. They are used for exploring areas far below the surface of the ocean. *Deep Flight* is a small, one-person submersible. Unlike submarines, it does not use **buoyancy tanks** to move up and down in the water. Instead, it has wings that help it "fly" through the sea.

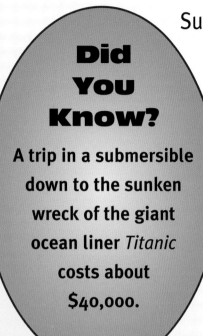

The main body is made of a light, strong material. It can stand up to the high pressure of the water outside the submersible.

Deep Flight has stubby wings and looks a lot like an airplane. Instead of lifting *Deep Flight* into the air, however, these wings help it glide down through the water to a great **depth**.

FACTS AND STATS

First Year: 1996

Origin: United States

Length:
13 feet (4 m)

Width:
7.9 feet (2.4 m)

Maximum Weight:
1.4 tons (1.3 m tons)

Load: 1 pilot

Engines:
Two electric motors,
each rated at 5 hp

Maximum Speed: 12 knots

Ascent Rate:
650 feet (198 m) per minute

Descent Rate:
492 feet (150 m) per minute

Maximum Depth:
3,281 feet (1,000 m)

Deep Flight has up to four cameras and six lights. The lights are needed for seeing deep below the surface, where it is very dark.

TALL SHIP

Today, airplanes can travel around the world in just two days. In 1768, however, British captain James Cook took almost three years to make the journey in his ship, the *Endeavour*. Workers began creating an almost exact **replica** of this **tall ship** in 1988. In 1994, it sailed around the world on the same route as the original ship.

Did You Know?

The original *Endeavour* was first used to carry coal. After its voyage around the world, it became a French whaling ship.

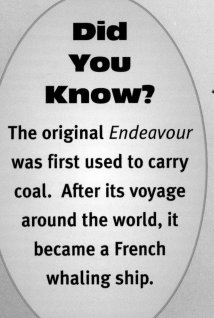

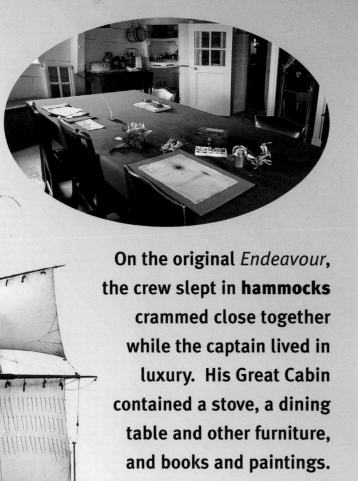

On the original *Endeavour*, the crew slept in **hammocks** crammed close together while the captain lived in luxury. His Great Cabin contained a stove, a dining table and other furniture, and books and paintings.

Each of the twelve sails has a special name. The small triangular sail at the front, for example, is called the jib. Unlike the original, the replica uses two engines in addition to wind power.

Extra wooden planks on the hull help prevent damage caused by **shipworms**. These pests eat away wood at an incredible rate in **tropical seas**.

RACING YACHT

Every year, the fastest yachts in the world compete against each other in a round-the-world yacht race. In 2002, eight yachts raced against each other for over nine months and traveled over 37,284 miles (60,000 km). The yacht *illbruck* won the race.

Did You Know?

The whole *illbruck* project — yacht, crew, backup team, equipment, training, transportation, and supplies — cost millions of dollars.

The yachts had to battle giant waves and howling **gales**. They also had to watch out for collisions with icebergs, whales, and each other!

Crew members pull the cables that control the sails by using high-speed **winches** with long handles. The height of the tallest mast is 85 feet (26 m).

The satellite communications center lets people on board communicate by telephone, e-mail, and video.

RESEARCH SHIP

The *James Clark Ross* is an incredibly strong ship that can smash its way through ice more than 6 feet (2 m) thick. This **research** ship is actually a huge floating **laboratory**. It is used for scientific research in the cold ocean waters around Antarctica.

The ship has five main laboratories, but more can be loaded on the deck in house-sized containers.

The main hull is made of very thick steel, so it can withstand collisions with ice and icebergs.

Did You Know?

The *James Clark Ross* has a system that rolls the ship from side to side to prevent the hull from being squeezed and cracked by ice.

FACTS AND STATS

First Year: 1990

Origin: Britain

Length: 325 feet (99 m)

Width: 62 feet (18.9 m)

Maximum Weight:
6,316 tons (5,732 m tons)

Fuel Capacity:
356,670 gallons
(1,350 cubic meters)

Load: 12 officers, 1 doctor, 31 scientists, and a crew of 15

Engines: Four Wartsilla engines delivering a total of 8,500 hp

Maximum Speed: 15.7 knots

The *James Clark Ross* measures depths and currents, and it also acts as a floating weather station. It even searches for strange creatures deep in the ocean.

FIREBOAT

Although ships are surrounded by water, they can still catch fire. Their engines and fuel might go up in flames, or they might be carrying **cargo** that is **flammable**, such as oil. Almost every big port has fireboats for handling emergencies. The Los Angeles Fireboat No. 2 is one of six fireboats used by the Los Angeles Fire Department.

All parts of the fireboat are fireproof, so it will not burst into flames while putting out a fire.

2 LOS ANGELES CITY FIRE D

When structures close to the water catch fire, fireboats are often used. To put out electrical fires, fireboats spray special foam instead of water.

FACTS AND STATS

First Year: 1925

Origin: United States

Length: 98 feet (30 m)

Width: 20 feet (6 m)

Maximum Weight:
168 tons (152 m tons)

Fuel Capacity:
2,590 gallons (9,801 l)

Load: 14 crew members

Engines:
Two Cummins V-12 engines, each rated at 700 hp; three Cummins inline-6 engines, each rated at 380 hp; and two Detroit V-12 engines, each rated at 525 hp

Maximum Speed: 17 knots

This fireboat has six water pumps. Each pump is powered by its own engine. The pumps suck in water from around the boat and send the water to the boat's water guns. The guns shoot powerful jets of water more than 455 feet (140 m) high.

AIRCRAFT CARRIER

Did You Know?

Every day, up to 20,000 meals are served to hungry sailors and the air crew on board the *Nimitz*.

Aircraft carriers such as the USS *Nimitz* are the largest warships ever built. The *Nimitz* is part of the U.S. Navy. It is like a floating airport — large numbers of military planes and helicopters use the ship for taking off and landing. The *Nimitz* has 3,360 sailors and 2,500 air crew members on board. The ship has more people than many small towns!

This ship carries up to 85 planes and 6 helicopters, along with pilots, a service crew, spare parts for the aircraft, and tools. Fuel for the aircraft is stored in tanks the size of swimming pools.

On the *Nimitz*, many people are needed to operate all of the ship's complicated equipment. This equipment includes computers, radar, and weapons such as missiles.

FACTS AND STATS

First Year: 1972

Origin: United States

Length: 1,093 feet (333 m)

Width: 134 feet (40.8 m)

Maximum Weight:
Over 110,200 tons
(100,000 m tons)

Load:
85 planes, 6 helicopters,
and a total crew of 5,860

Engines: Two nuclear reactors powering four steam turbines to produce 260,000 hp

Maximum Speed:
Over 30 knots

The *Nimitz* is almost as long as the Empire State Building is tall.

SUPERTANKER

The biggest ships in the world are the giant tankers that carry **crude oil**. This precious cargo is used to make gasoline and other fuels, and it is also used to make plastics, paints, and hundreds of other products. The supertanker *Jahre Viking* is over 1/4 mile (400 m) long. Once this massive ship gets going, it needs 5 miles (8 km) to come to a stop!

Did You Know?

If the Eiffel Tower was laid down on its side, it would fit on the deck of the *Jahre Viking*!

Most of the *Jahre Viking* is controlled by computer, so it needs only thirty-five to forty crew members. They live in the **stern** of the ship, in a structure that is several stories high.

FACTS AND STATS

First Year: 1979

Origin: Japan

Length: 1,504 feet (458 m)

Width: 226 feet (69 m)

Maximum Weight:
714,046 tons
(647,955 m tons)

Fuel Capacity:
5,285 gallons (20,000 l)

Load:
4,240,865 barrels of oil

Crew: 35 to 40 people

Engines: One steam
turbine rated at 50,019 hp

Maximum Speed: 10 knots

At an oil terminal, oil is pumped into tankers through pipes. The oil is pumped off again at an **oil refinery**.

Walking the length of the *Jahre Viking's* deck can take a long time, so crew members sometimes use bicycles to get around!

JET SKI

Jet skis are like snowmobiles for the water. Instead of zooming across snow, they blast across waves. A jet ski gets its power from a strong jet of water that shoots out the back. On the Polaris Virage TX, riders can perform all kinds of stunts, including somersaults! If a rider falls off a jet ski, the craft stops immediately.

Did You Know?

The jet ski was developed in the late 1960s. An American motorcycle rider named Clay Jacobson came up with the idea. At the time, he was working for Kawasaki, a Japanese motorcycle company.

The jet ski's engine turns a fanlike device. This device sucks water in through a large opening and blasts it out the back as a fast, narrow jet of water.

Jet ski riders can perform amazing turns and jumps, and they can also dive into the water. The Virage TX can reach speeds of 52 knots, which equals 60 miles (96 km) per hour.

A rider steers by turning the handlebars. The jet of water in the back can shoot forward to slow down or reverse the jet ski.

FERRY

Stena Line is a company that operates **ferries** in Europe and the United Kingdom. *Stena Discovery* is one of the company's HSS (High-speed Sea Service) ferries. These large car ferries are **catamarans** — they have twin hulls that cut through waves to provide a smooth, fast ride.

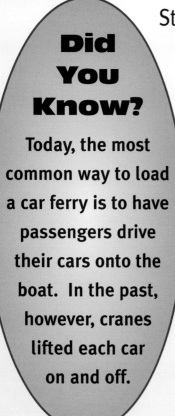

Did You Know?

Today, the most common way to load a car ferry is to have passengers drive their cars onto the boat. In the past, however, cranes lifted each car on and off.

The hulls of *Stena Discovery* are mostly made of **aluminum**. This metal is very light and does not rust in salt water.

Catamaran ferries operate around the world. The catamaran pictured above serves passengers traveling in the Caribbean Sea. The boat can hold more than 370 cars and 1,500 passengers and has many lounge areas, restaurants, and bars.

FACTS AND STATS

First Year: 1997

Origin: Finland

Length:
415 feet (126.5 m)

Width:
131 feet (40 m)

Maximum Weight:
1,653 tons (1,500 m tons)

Load:
1,500 passengers
and 375 cars

Engines:
Two GE LM2500 gas turbines, each rated at 27,490 hp, and two GE LM1600 gas turbines, each rated at 18,103 hp

Maximum Speed: 40 knots

Stena Discovery **has four huge engines that produce an incredible amount of power.**

LUXURY LINER

The World is a different kind of luxury liner. On this ship, people live in permanent homes! For a large amount of money, you can buy a set of rooms and live on the ship year round. It travels to many exciting events around the world, including **Carnival** in Rio de Janeiro, Brazil, and an auto race in Monaco.

Did You Know?

The luxurious homes on *The World* **cost millions of dollars.**

The ship has twelve decks. It contains gyms, swimming pools, and tennis courts, as well as restaurants, theaters, cinemas, a nightclub, and a casino.

On *The World*, people are **residents**, not passengers. The ship has 110 main residences and 88 apartments that can be rented out to guests.

FACTS AND STATS

First Year: 2001

Origin: Norway

Length: 644.4 feet (196.4 m)

Width: 97.8 feet (29.8 m)

Maximum Weight:
47,963 tons
(43,524 m tons)

Fuel Capacity:
303,830 gallons
(1,150 cubic m)

Load: 976 residents, guests, and crew members

Engines: Two Wartsila engines rated at 7,402 hp

Maximum Speed: 18.5 knots

The hull of the ship is made of huge pieces of steel that were put into place with giant cranes.

RESCUE BOAT

Did You Know?

In the seas around Britain, lifeboats head out on rescue missions fifteen to twenty times a day.

The ocean can be a dangerous place. During bad storms, when ocean waves can reach incredible heights, even large ships might need help. In Britain, the brave crews of the Royal National Lifeboat Institution (RNLI) are always ready to rescue sailors in trouble. The British call their rescue boats lifeboats. This powerful Trent-class lifeboat can handle the roughest seas.

The hull of the lifeboat is made from a combination of **carbon fiber** and different plastics. This hull is light but strong, and it will never rust.

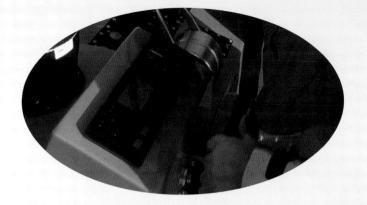

The crew on the lifeboat uses special radar and radio equipment to track ships that are in trouble.

FACTS AND STATS

First Year: 1994

Origin: Britain

Length:
46.9 feet (14.3 m)

Maximum Weight:
30.3 tons (27.5 m tons)

Fuel Capacity:
900 gallons (3,406 l)

Load: 10 people

Engines:
Two MAN engines,
each rated at 808 hp

Maximum Speed:
Over 25 knots

14-01
Lifeboat

The survivor's cabin has seats for ten people. It also has heaters, dry clothes, and a **galley**.

GLOSSARY

aluminum: a light metal that does not rust.

bulkheads: on a boat, special walls that create watertight compartments.

buoyancy tanks: tanks that are filled with water to make a submarine dive and emptied of water to make it rise.

carbon fiber: a threadlike material that is light but very strong.

cargo: a shipment that a vehicle carries from one place to another.

Carnival: a Catholic holiday that is celebrated with a big festival in Rio de Janeiro, Brazil, and other places.

catamarans: boats with two smaller hulls instead of one large hull.

crude oil: oil from the ground that can be turned into gasoline, plastics, and other products.

currents: areas of an ocean where the water moves constantly in the same direction.

depth: the distance downward from the surface of the water.

ferries: boats that carry people and vehicles from one place to another.

flammable: able to catch on fire very easily.

gales: extremely strong winds.

galley: the kitchen area on a boat.

hammocks: beds made of cloth or netting that hang from supports.

horsepower: a unit of measurement for an engine's power that was originally based on the pulling strength of a horse.

hull: the main body of a boat or ship, consisting of the bottom and the sides below the deck.

knots: units of measurement for the speed of a boat or ship. One knot equals 1.15 miles (1.85 km) per hour.

laboratory: a place used for scientific experiments and research.

linen: a kind of cloth that is strong and smooth.

oil refinery: a place that can turn crude oil into fuels, such as gasoline, and other products.

radar: a system that finds objects, such as icebergs or boats lost at sea, by sending out invisible radio waves.

replica: a copy of something, such as an old ship, that has the same features as the original.

research: the study of something, usually by collecting facts and conducting experiments.

residents: the people living permanently in a particular place.

roll cage: a metal framework that protects a drag boat driver if the boat rolls over during a crash.

satellites: machines that circle Earth in space and are used for many purposes, such as for helping people find their way on the ground and for sending signals for telephones, computers, and other equipment.

shipworms: clams resembling worms that damage wood in water.

stern: the rear part of a boat or ship.

tall ship: a large sailing ship that has two or more masts.

tropical seas: ocean waters in the warm regions of Earth near the Equator.

winches: machines that pull or lift things by winding a cable or rope around a wheel.

INDEX